D0230990

The Usborne
First Book of Art

Rosie Dickins

Designed by Nicola Butler

With cartoons by Philip Hopman

Withdrawn
from Stock

3 8002 02208 928 0

Contents

Coventry City Council	
COU	
3 8002 02208 928 0	
Askews & Holts	Feb-2015
J700	£7.99

About this book

This book is full of art to look at and arty
things to make. You can meet imaginary monsters
and explore exotic landscapes - then you can have
a go at making your own versions, based on
similar ideas and methods.

What you need

You can make everything using ordinary, everyday materials (see the list below).
Don't forget to spread out old newspaper before starting anything messy.

Useful things

- Paper
- Cardboard
- Tissue paper
- Paints
- Brushes
- Crayons
- Pens
- Scissors
- Craft glue (PVA)
- Leaves
- Sponge
- Yarn
- Sequins
- Old magazines

▶Faces

Looking at pictures, you often find faces looking back at you – faces of real people from the past, or startling imaginary faces.

This painting shows a girl in fancy dress, with a silky turban and a huge pearl earring. It's so lifelike, it could almost be a photograph.

Before photography, paintings like this were the only way to record how people looked.

Girl with a Turban (about 1665) by Jan Vermeer. No one knows who the girl was, though some experts think she may have been the artist's daughter.

Nusch (1937) by Pablo Picasso. Nusch was an actress and model, and a friend of the artist.

This picture is full of wonky shapes and funny colours. Can you see a sideways view of a face? And a front view? It's as if the woman kept fidgeting while she was being painted.

Mbuya mask, possibly about 100 years old, by an unknown artist from Zaire, Africa.

This wooden mask was carved to look like a face. It comes from Africa, where masks were used in traditional ceremonies and dances.

▶ Funny face

Summer (1573) by Giuseppe Arcimboldo

How many different fruits can you see in this painting?

Can you spot where the artist put in the date?

Look closely at this painting. Do you see a face, or a lot of fruits and vegetables? It's a kind of puzzle picture, painted to amuse the artist's rich clients.

You can make a
puzzle picture from
old magazines.

1. Cut out a big
face, and smaller
plants and fruits.

Try to
match
shapes.

2. Arrange the
plants and fruits
on top of the face.

Families

Family pictures often show the relationships between people, as well as what the people looked like.

This sculpture shows a man and woman holding their children. The smooth, overlapping curves create a sense of togetherness. And the rich bronze colour adds a feeling of warmth, too.

Family Group (1947) by Henry Moore

The Family of King Philip IV (1656) by Diego Velasquez

Look closely... can you spot two people reflected in a mirror? It's the king and queen.

This painting shows the Spanish royal family. It's more like a family snapshot than a formal portrait. A young princess poses for the artist, surrounded by her ladies in waiting, curious courtiers and a sleepy dog.

Family tree

The Family Tree of Rene II, Duke of Lorraine
(15th century), by an unknown artist

Another way of recording family relationships is a family tree. This 600-year-old drawing shows the family tree of a French duke.

The duke lies at the bottom, with his relatives on the branches above him. The duke is biggest, to show he is most important.

Grandma
Mary

Grandpa
Oliver

Grandma
Rose

Grandpa
Evan

Dad

Mum

Me

Make a picture of your own family tree.

1. Paint a tree. Cut some paper leaves. Glue on.

2. Make an apple for each member of your family. Glue on.

Put your apple near the bottom of the tree.

Animals

There are all kinds of animals in art, from fierce tigers and cheeky monkeys to cartoon mice – as you can see over the following pages.

Hippo statue (about 4,000 years old) by an unknown Eygptian artist

This hippo statue comes from Ancient Egypt and is decorated with flowers. It was meant to bring good luck.

In the painting below, jagged shapes and strong colours help show the tiger's power.

Tiger (1912) by Franz Marc

In this jungle painting, monkeys swing from trees and feast on bright oranges. The leafy background looks lush and inviting.

Exotic Landscape (1910) by Henri Rousseau

The artist, Henri Rousseau, had never been anywhere near a jungle – but he spent ages imagining what it might be like.

▶ Stand-up hippo

Here's how to make and decorate your own hippo statue, based on the Ancient Egyptian one.

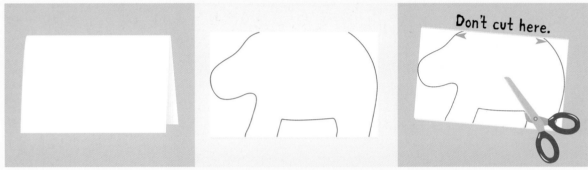

Don't cut here.

1. Fold a piece of thin cardboard in half.

2. Draw a hippo. Make it touch top and bottom.

3. Cut it out. Don't cut the top edge.

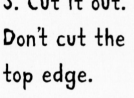

4. Glue on tissue paper shapes. Leave to dry.

5. Use a pen to add eyes, nose and ears.

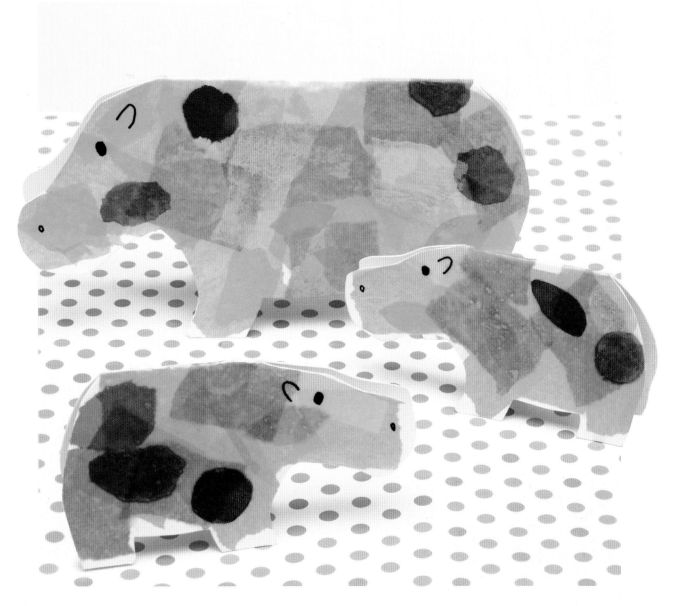

Use smaller pieces of cardboard to make baby hippos.

▶ Jungle bird

You can create an imaginary jungle, like Rousseau, by inventing a wild bird and using real leaves to add the background.

1. Paint a bird body and head. Add a long tail.

2. Make two handprints for the wings.

3. Dot on a white eye with a black middle.

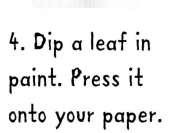

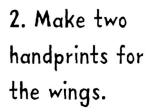

4. Dip a leaf in paint. Press it onto your paper.

5. Peel it off. Do the same with more leaves.

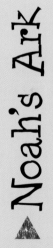

Noah's Ark

The Entry of the Animals into Noah's Ark (1613) by Jan Brueghel

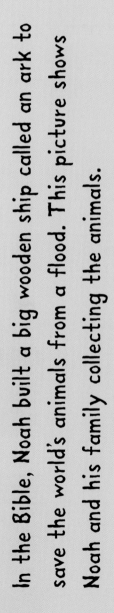

In the Bible, Noah built a big wooden ship called an ark to save the world's animals from a flood. This picture shows Noah and his family collecting the animals.

Each creature is painted in amazing detail. Their fur and feathers look so soft, you could almost stroke them. They were based on real animals from a wealthy duke's private zoo.

Look at the picture closely...

Can you spot Noah with his long white beard?

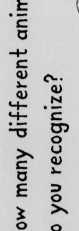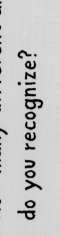

How many different animals do you recognize?

Noah had to collect a pair of each animal. How many pairs can you find?

21

Funny animals

Cartoon animals usually have simple shapes, so they can be drawn over and over. Funny, exaggerated faces give them extra character.

This picture of a dog uses bright colour and bold outlines to grab your attention.

The artist, Andy Warhol, loved little dogs – which may be why he called this "You Are So Little".

You Are So Little (1958) by Andy Warhol

Foss Dancing
(1894) by Edward Lear

Foss Standing
(1894)

Artist Edward Lear had a cat called Old Foss. He liked to draw Foss in funny poses, with huge eyes and a short, stumpy tail.

Walt Disney made his fortune with a cartoon mouse. He was going to call him Mortimer, but his wife suggested Mickey - and the rest is history.

Mickey Mouse
was created in 1928
by Walt Disney
and Ub Iwerks.

Look closely at all the cartoons... notice how some have scratchy lines, and some have smooth ones.

▶ Cartoon cats

Lear sketched his cartoon cats in pen. You can do the same, using splodges of paint to give them shape.

Don't worry about being too neat.

1. Paint several blobs of thin, watery paint.

2. Add spots and stripes. Let the paint dry.

3. Use a felt pen to outline the ears and head.

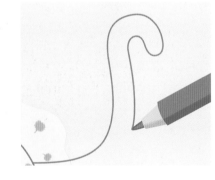

4. Outline the body and feet. Add a tail.

5. Draw the face. Add whiskers.

Try out
different
poses.

▶ Stories

Every picture tells a
story – but some pictures
are made specially to
illustrate a particular
story or poem.

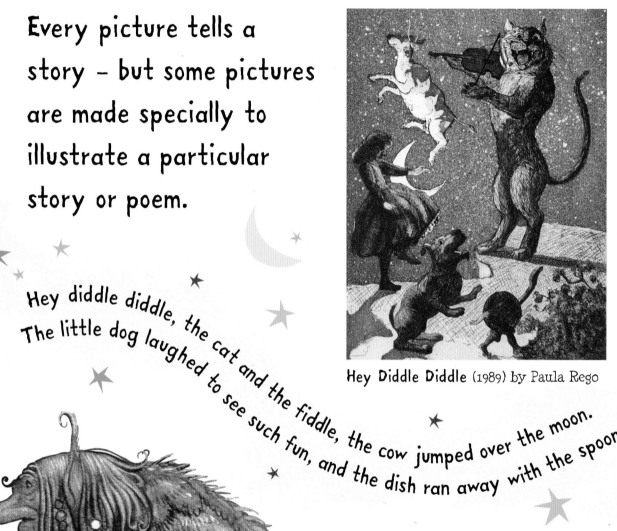

Hey Diddle Diddle (1989) by Paula Rego

Hey diddle diddle, the cat and the fiddle, the cow jumped over the moon.
The little dog laughed to see such fun, and the dish ran away with the spoon.

This hairy monster
comes from a Swedish
fairy tale about trolls.

Detail from **The Princess and
the Trolls** (1913) by John Bauer

Rustam (16th century) by an unknown Indian artist

This picture was painted to illustrate an ancient Persian tale. Prince Rustam, the hero, sits on the elephant on the left. His grandfather faces him on another elephant. The rich decorations show how important they are.

▶ Decorated elephant

You could make up a story about your own elephant ride –
then make and decorate the elephant you imagined.

1. Draw a big oval body. Add two stumpy legs.

2. Add a long trunk and a short tail. Cut him out.

3. Cut out a big ear, a curvy tusk and toes.

Tusk

Ear

Toes

Glue under here

4. Glue down the front edge of the ear. Then glue on the tusk and toes. Use bits of paper and sequins to decorate.

Saint George and the Dragon

This painting was made over 500 years ago to illustrate a famous story about a dragon. You can read the story below.

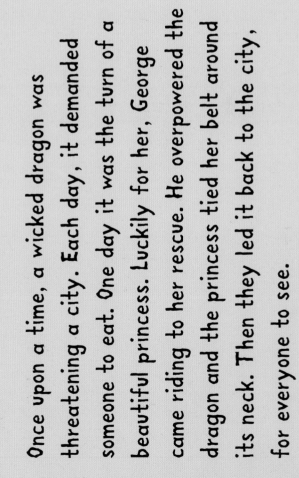

Once upon a time, a wicked dragon was threatening a city. Each day, it demanded someone to eat. One day it was the turn of a beautiful princess. Luckily for her, George came riding to her rescue. He overpowered the dragon and the princess tied her belt around its neck. Then they led it back to the city, for everyone to see.

Look closely at the painting... notice the dragon's big, pointy teeth and claws. But the princess doesn't seem afraid – she has him tamely on a leash.

Saint George and the Dragon (about 1470) by Paulo Uccello

▶ Handprint dragon

Here's how to paint a dragon like the one Saint George had to fight. See how fierce you can make your dragon look.

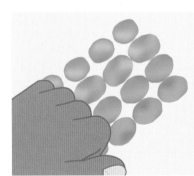  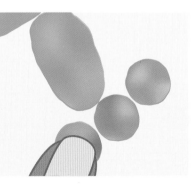

1. Make a row of prints with the front of your fist.

2. Turn your paper. Paint the neck and head.

3. Give him two legs and feet. Add a twisty tail.

4. For wings, add two overlapping handprints.

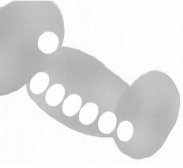

5. Dot on white eyes and teeth. Leave to dry.

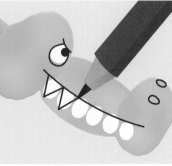

6. Use a pen to finish the face and add claws.

 # Weather

Many artists have made pictures inspired by the weather, from summer sunshine to dramatic storms – as you can see over the following pages.

Boating on the Seine (1879-80) by Auguste Renoir

This scene glows with sunlight. Notice how little dabs of orange and yellow make the blue water seem to sparkle.

Winter (about 1840) by Utagawa Kunisada

Does this picture make you feel cold? It's full of cold-looking colours - snowy white and chilly greys. Even the woman's skirt is an icy blue.

This rainbow picture was painted in bright dots of colour. Look at it from further away... do you notice the dots less?

Entrance to the Port of Honfleur (1899) by Paul Signac

Watery rainbow

The rainbow on the previous page was made by mixing coloured dots. You can also make one by mixing runny paints.

1. Draw a row of houses and trees in crayon.

2. Brush clean water all over your paper.

3. Make some runny red, yellow and blue paint.

4. Paint curved lines of red and yellow in the sky.

5. Let the paint run together. Add a blue line.

6. Fill the rest of the sky with splodges of blue.

Where the red and yellow mix, you get orange.

Yellow and blue mix to make green.

Sunlit lilies

Water Lilies (1916-19) by Claude Monet

This peaceful lily pond belonged to artist Claude Monet. He painted it hundreds of times, trying to capture the changing effects of sunlight on water.

Monet painted with big, bold brush strokes, sometimes leaving bare patches. It's like a quick impression – and this kind of art is known as Impressionism.

Look at this close-up... can you follow the sweeping, swirling lines left by the artist's brush?

Monet designed the pond himself, including a Japanese-style bridge, which he also painted.

39

▶ Stormy seas

Artist Joseph Turner painted this picture after being on a ship in a storm. He said he had to be tied to the mast so he wasn't swept overboard.

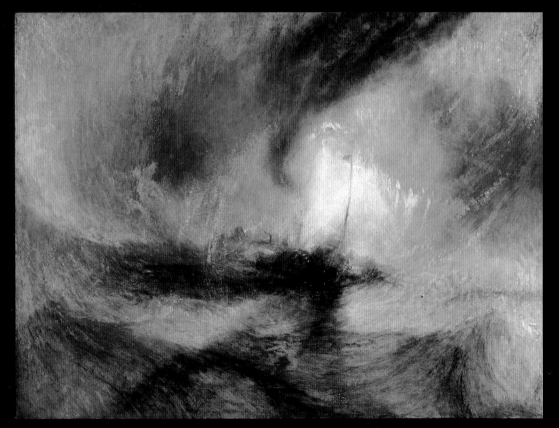

Snow Storm (1842) by Joseph Turner

The picture is blurred with spray and foam. Critics called it "soapsuds and whitewash". Look closely... can you make out a ship in the middle?

Imagine being in a storm, like Turner, with thundery clouds and crashing waves. Then create it on paper...

1. Tear lots of dark clouds. Glue them down.

2. Cut out big, curvy waves. Glue them below.

3. Flick some white paint over the top, for rain.

▶ Flowers

Flowers are a popular choice for pictures – sometimes just because they're pretty.
But sometimes, flowers carry hidden meanings...

Footbridge over a River (1800s) by Utagawa Hiroshige

This picture comes from Japan. It shows spring blossom, which is celebrated in Japan as a symbol of things coming to life again after the winter.

The artist carved the picture on wooden blocks. Then he coated the blocks with ink and printed them onto paper.

Carnation, Lily, Lily, Rose (1885-86) by John Singer Sargent

According to tradition, lilies mean purity, and roses and
carnations mean love. All of them appear in this magical
twilight garden, where two girls are lighting lanterns.
The artist made sure he painted everything at dusk,
to get the colours exactly right.

▶ More flowers

Sunflowers (1888) by Vincent van Gogh

Artist Vincent van Gogh painted these sunflowers for a friend, using lots of thick, sunny yellow paint. For van Gogh, yellow was the colour of happiness and friendship.

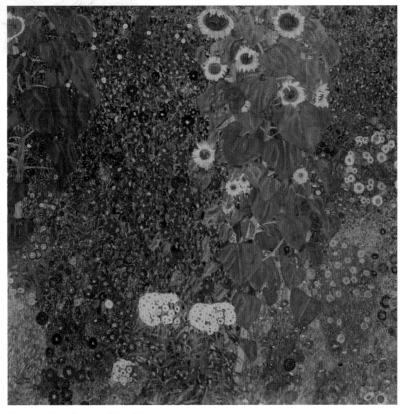

Farm Garden with Flowers (1906) by Gustav Klimt

This picture is crammed with flowers, showing the richness of nature. The artist used every colour of the rainbow to paint it.

Mastaba (1989) by Jean-Pierre Raynaud

This giant red flowerpot was made by a French artist. It's twice as tall as a person. Can you imagine what it would look like with giant flowers growing in it?

▶ Paper blossom

Some artists don't just paint flowers, they make sculptures too. Here's a way to make a paper sculpture of Japanese-style blossom.

1. Lay two squares of tissue paper together.

2. Fold them in half, and then in half again.

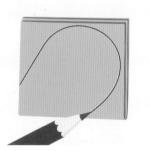

Tie a knot under the flower, to keep it in place.

3. Draw a petal in the corner. Cut out and unfold.

4. Use a blunt needle to thread the flower onto yarn.

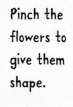

Pinch the flowers to give them shape.

5. Thread on more flowers. Add some paper leaves, too.

▶ Printed petals

Van Gogh made his sunflowers out of bright, thick layers of paint. Here's how you can do the same using printing.

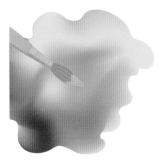

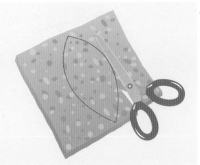

1. Mix your paint with a little flour to thicken it.

2. Cut a petal shape from a thin piece of sponge.

3. Dip the sponge in paint. Print a ring of petals.

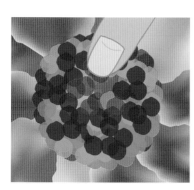

4. Use your fingertip to fill in the middle.

5. Dip a leaf in paint. Print it next to the flower. Add more flowers and leaves.

 Places

Many artists make art inspired by places, whether real or imaginary – as you can see over the next few pages.

This painting shows a busy street in a factory town in northern England. You can just see a tall factory chimney in the distance.

Look closely... can you spot three little dogs among the people?

An Organ Grinder (1934) by Laurence Stephen Lowry

Nichols Canyon (1980) by David Hockney

Here, a road winds through the Hollywood Hills in California.
Bold, zingy colours make everything look bright and hot.

Imaginary places

This picture shows a strange, dreamy sort of place.
The artist painted it in a very detailed way, to make it
seem more real – but there is no way it could actually exist.

Look at
the painting
closely... do you
see trees or
giant leaves?
And someone riding
among them?

Most of the picture shows a dark,
night-time view of a house in a park.
But the sky is a light, day-time
blue. The result is meant to feel
startling and 'surreal' – meaning
like the weird reality you get in
some dreams. This kind of art is
known as Surrealism.

The Mysterious Barricades (1961) by René Magritte

▶ Outdoor art

Some artists don't just paint places – they make art out of the place itself, using leaves, stones, grass, or whatever they find there.

These scarlet leaves were put together by an artist. But he knew the pattern wouldn't last. Soon, water washed the leaves away. Now, this photo is the only trace of his work.

Hole in Leaves Sinking (1987) by Andy Goldsworthy

Try making a temporary picture
out of things you can find outdoors.

1. Collect things
to use, such as
pebbles or twigs.

2. Draw a simple
shape. Arrange the
things around it.

▶ Patterns

Some artists make pictures of colours, shapes and patterns, instead of real-life things. This is known as 'abstract' art.

This abstract picture was inspired by the sun and moon. There are lots of round sun and moon-like shapes. And the bright colours almost seem to glow with light.

Simultaneous Contrasts:
Sun and Moon (1912-13) by Robert Delaunay

What happens when you look at this picture?
To many people, the pattern appears to flicker and move.

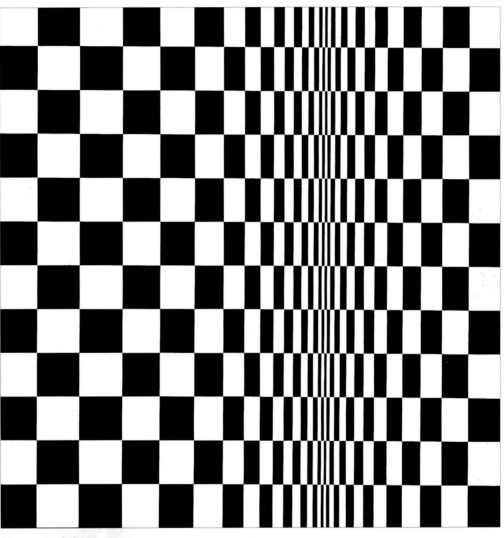

Movement in Squares (1961) by Bridget Riley

Look closely... do the squares change shape? And do some
of the white squares look brighter than others?

▶ Abstract weaving

Abstract art often uses bold, repeated patterns. You can make your own abstract pattern by weaving paper strips together.

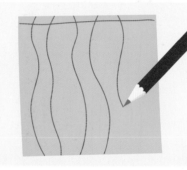

Don't cut here.

1. Take three pieces of paper in different colours.

2. Draw wavy lines across one piece, like this.

3. Cut along the waves. Don't cut right to the edge.

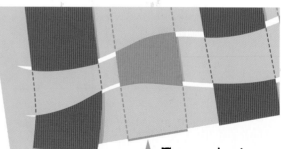

Tape under here.

4. Cut the other pieces of paper into strips.

5. Weave the strips under and over the waves. Turn the weaving over. Tape the ends.

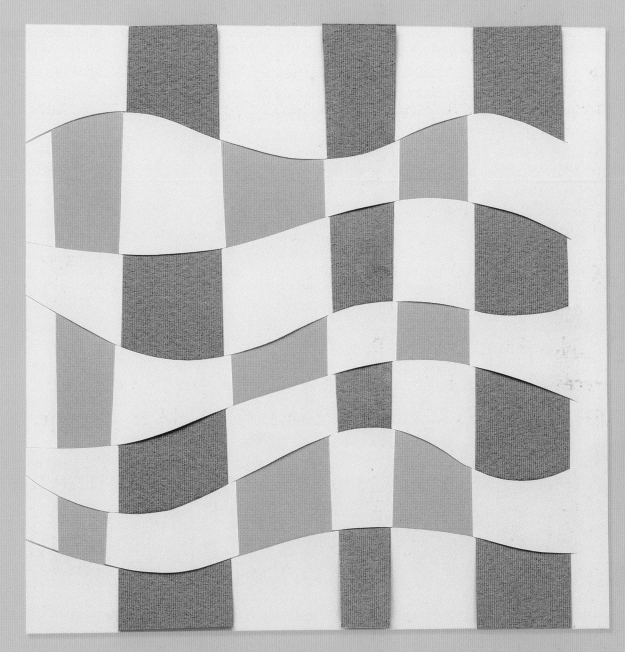

Try using different colours of paper for different effects.

▶ Spattery art

Frost (2001) by Howard Hodgkin

This abstract picture is made up of chilly blue streaks and icy white spatters. Does it remind you of anything? The title tells you what the artist had in mind.

You can get a similar streaky, spattery effect by using glue and watercolour paint.

The gluey parts will stay white.

1. Mix craft glue and water. Spatter it over your paper.

2. Let it dry. Then, mix some watery paint.

3. Quickly sponge streaks of paint over the glue.

Art quiz

Can you use your new knowledge of art to solve these puzzles? (Look back through the book if you need to refresh your memory.)

Artists at work

Look at these patches of paint.
Can you tell which artists have been working here?

Lost characters

These characters are lost.
Do you know which pictures they belong to?

a  b c

Map mystery

a

Do you remember which countries these works of art come from?

b  c

Turn the page for the answers...

Art quiz answers

Artists at work: (a) Paul Signac, (b) Vincent van Gogh, (c) Claude Monet, (d) David Hockney.
Lost characters: (a) The Family of Philip IV, (b) Rustam, (c) Exotic Landscape.
Map mystery: (a) Japan, (b) Egypt, (c) Africa.

Acknowledgements

Picture research by Ruth King
Project artwork by Katie Lovell, Antonia Miller, Abigail Brown, Nicola Butler,
Helen Edmonds, Nancy Leschnikoff and Jessica Johnson
Project steps by Jo Moore, photography by Howard Allman
Edited by Jane Chisholm and Jenny Tyler

Every effort has been made to trace the copyright holders of the material in this book. If any rights have been omitted, the publishers offer their sincere apologies and will rectify this in any subsequent editions following notification. The publishers are grateful to the following organisations and individuals for their contributions and permission to reproduce material:
Cover: **Exotic Landscape** by Rousseau, see credit for pages 14-15. Pages 6-7: **Girl with a Turban** by Vermeer © Photo Scala, Florence. **Portrait of Nusch** by Picasso © Succession Picasso/DACS 2007/Musee Picasso, Paris/Giraudon/Bridgeman Art Library. **Mbuya mask** from Zaire © Private Collection/Heini Schneebeli/Bridgeman Art Library. Pages 8-9: **Summer** by Arcimboldo © Louvre, Paris/ Lauros/Giraudon/Bridgeman Art Library. Pages 10-11: **Family Group** by Moore, reproduced by permission of the Henry Moore Foundation, digital image © Christie's Images/CORBIS. **Family of Philip IV** by Velasquez © Photo Scala, Florence. Pages 12-13: **Genealogy of Rene II, Duke of Lorraine** © Bibliotheque de l'Institut de France, Paris/ Archives Charmet/Bridgeman Art Library. Pages 14-15: **Tiger** by Marc © Stadtische Galerie im Lenbachhaus, Munich/Interfoto/ Bridgeman Art Library. **Statuette of a Hippopotamus** © Metropolitan Museum of Art/Art Resource/Scala, Florence. **Exotic Landscape** by Rousseau © Norton Simon Collection, Pasadena/Bridgeman Art Library. Pages 20-21: **Entry of the Animals into Noah's Ark** by Brueghel © The J. Paul Getty Museum, Los Angeles. Pages 22-23: **You Are So Little** by Warhol © Andy Warhol Foundation for the Visual Arts/Corbis. **Foss dancing** and **Foss standing** by Edward Lear, Opie PP583, p.138 (ref. 4544) and p.139 (ref. 4491) © Bodleian Library, University of Oxford. **Mickey Mouse** by Disney © Disney Enterprises, Inc. Pages 26-27: **Hey Diddle Diddle** by Rego © Paula Rego/Leeds Museums and Galleries (City Art Gallery)/Bridgeman Art Library. **Princess and the Trolls** (detail) by Bauer © Nationalmuseum, Stockholm/Bridgeman Art Library. **First Meeting of Rustam and his Grandfather, Sam** © Musee Conde, Chantilly/Giraudon/Bridgeman Art Library. Pages 30-31: **St. George and the Dragon** by Uccello © National Gallery, London 2007. Pages 34-35: **Boating on the Seine** by Renoir © National Gallery, London 2007. **Entrance to the Port of Honfleur** by Signac © Indianapolis Museum of Art, USA/Holliday Collection/ Bridgeman Art Library. **Winter** by Kunisada © Musee Claude Monet, Giverny/Giraudon/Bridgeman Art Library. Pages 38-39: **Water Lilies** by Monet © Musee Marmottan, Paris/Bridgeman Art Library. Pages 40-41: **Snow Storm – Steam-Boat off a Harbour's Mouth** by Turner © Tate, London 2007. Pages 42-43: **Footbridge over River with Wisteria in full bloom** by Hiroshige © British Library, London/ British Library Board. All Rights Reserved/Bridgeman Art Library. **Carnation, Lily, Lily, Rose** by Sargent © Tate, London 2007. Pages 44-45: **Sunflowers** by van Gogh © National Gallery, London 2007. **Farm Garden with Flowers** by Klimt © Osterreichische Galerie Belvedere, Vienna/Bridgeman Art Library. **View of a Red Pot in the Mastaba** by Raynaud © M&Y Di Folco/Jean-Pierre Raynaud/ ADAGP, Paris/DACS, London 2007, photo courtesy JGM Galerie, Paris. Pages 50-51: **Organ Grinder** by Lowry © The Estate of L.S. Lowry, 2007/Manchester Art Gallery, UK/Bridgeman Art Library. **Nichols Canyon** by Hockney © David Hockney. Pages 52-53: **Mysterious Barricades** by Magritte © ADAGP, Paris and DACS, London 2007/Private Collection/Bridgeman Art Library. Pages 54-55: **Hole in Leaves Sinking** by Goldsworthy © Andy Goldsworthy. Pages 56-57: **Simultaneous Contrasts: Sun and Moon** by Delaunay © L&M Services B.V. The Hague 20070404/Museum of Modern Art, New York/Scala, Florence. **Movement in Squares** by Riley © 2007 Bridget Riley. All Rights Reserved. Pages 60-61: **Frost** by Hodgkin © Howard Hodgkin. Pages 62-63: Details, please see previous credits.
Usborne Publishing Ltd has paid DACS' visual creators for the use of their artistic works.

This edition first published in 2014 by Usborne Publishing Ltd, 83-85 Saffron Hill, London, EC1N 8RT, England. www.usborne.com
Copyright © 2014, 2007 Usborne Publishing Ltd. The name Usborne and the devices ♀☉ are Trade Marks of Usborne Publishing Ltd.
All rights reserved. No part of this publication may be reproduced, stored in a retrieval system, or transmitted in any form or by any means, electronic, mechanical, photocopying, recording or otherwise without the prior permission of the publisher. UKE.